Briana Hernandez
& Sophia Hernandez

Samson and Ivy

Bumblebee
Books

A CIP catalogue record for this title is
available from the British Library.

ISBN: 978-1-83934-561-6

Bumblebee Books is an imprint of
Olympia Publishers.

First Published in 2023

Bumblebee Books
Tallis House
2 Tallis Street
London
EC4Y 0AB

Printed in Great Britain

Dedication

We dedicate this book to the future generations of our family.

Samson and Ivy look nothing alike

They are two unique doggies

Ivy has spots

Samson has a mane.

They are very different

but also, the same

Ivy loves to run,

Samson loves to sleep

His bark is a roar

While hers is a peep

Ivy is fast

Samson is strong

How can opposites always get along?

They both love to play

and share treats
with one another

They come from two
different mommies

But are like sister
and brother!

Their outsides do not match

But their insides do!

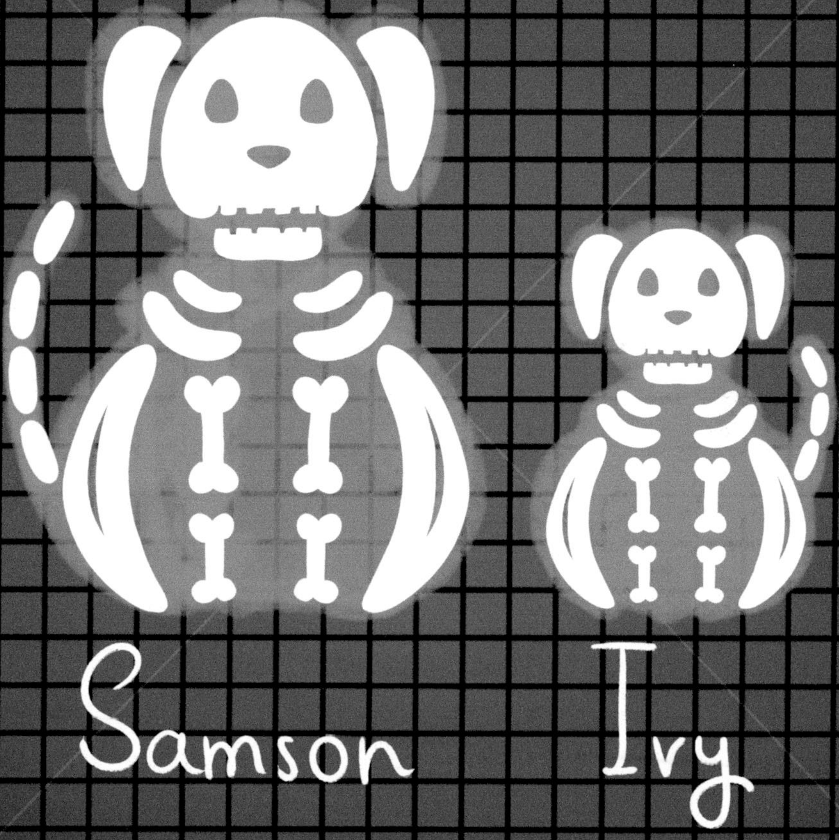

Samson
& Ivy

That's all that matters

In a best friend for you

About the Authors

Briana and Sophia Hernandez are identical twin sisters born in Charleston, South Carolina and raised in Irving, TX. The authors are both Medical Doctors, elder sisters to five siblings, and dog Mommy's to two unique pups. As identical twins and the best of friends, Briana and Sophia have personally known what it is like to be similar, but also very different. Considering this, it has been their lifelong dream to help influence and encourage equality and unity no matter the circumstance. Their mission to promote accepting, kind, undiscriminating behaviors in children and their families have remained steadfast.

Acknowledgements

Thank you to our four parents for always being so encouraging and uplifting of our dreams. Thank you to our five younger siblings for motivating us to create an exciting learning environment for younger generations to come. Thank you to our two dogs, Samson & Ivy with whom we owe this narrative to; you both have filled our hearts with abundant love beyond measure.